SEVEN NETWORKING SECRETS FOR JOBSEEKERS

HOW TO GET HIRED, GET A PROMOTION, AND GET A RAISE - EVEN IF YOU STINK AT RESUME RRITING, HATE THE INTERNET, AND HAVE BEEN OUT OF WORK FOR YEARS

JONATHAN GREEN

FOREWORD BY GREIG WELLS

My name is Greig Wells. I'm one of the biggest trainers in the world for job seekers. Using the power of LinkedIn, I have helped over one hundred thousand people get back to work over the past decade. For a long time, I was a corporate recruiter, but I was so tired of working for faceless corporations. My true passion has always been to help other people just like me get back to work so that they can support their families.

I'm always looking for ways to help people get back on their feet, and when Jonathan asked me to write the foreword to this book I was honored. Jonathan walked up to me at a conference, and within two months I was flying him across the country to coach me on his techniques. He is such an amazing guy that our relationship went beyond pure business, and for two years we were roommates. I taught him everything I know about LinkedIn and building a business, and he taught me his powerful networking secrets.

Jonathan is one of the greatest networkers I've ever met, and his understanding of the way people think and interact is nothing short of staggering. Since spending time with him, my business has doubled in size, and I have forged partnerships with people that I never believed possible, including Tony Robbins. Working with one of my heroes and speaking on his stage was one of the greatest moments in my life, and Jonathan played a critical role in getting me there.

So many job seekers are stuck following the conventional path. They send their resumes out only after they see jobs posted on the Internet. They are often showing up far after all the best jobs have been snapped up. The competition is getting tougher, and people need an edge. I can't wait to share this book with my audience. The techniques in here are nothing short of pure gold. Jonathan breaks down his networking strategy into seven simple steps. Instead of waiting for opportunities, you can connect with decision-makers before the competition shows up. Imagine being the only person to interview for a job. How much easier would it be to get the salary we both know you deserve?

I wouldn't be able to write the foreword for a book that I didn't believe in. Not only have I been on the receiving end of Jonathan's networking skills, but I have also used them to further my career. This book is a powerful way to get back to work and find a job that pays what you deserve. The strategy within is life-changing. Spend an afternoon reading this book and spend the rest of your life reaping the benefits. If you are tired of trudging from interview to interview and just want a job that gets you excited to wake up in the morning, then this book is essential. Stop reading this foreword and get to the good stuff right now!

Greig Wells
BeFoundJobs.com

JOIN THE TRIBE

When you have the work and knowledge of hundreds of REAL men and women living in real freedom, it's hard NOT to believe in yourself, and it's hard to fail.

If you're serious about have your own support network, I'd like you to join the Serve No Master Tribe. This group is free - but it's private. I don't post the link on my website, I don't share it in my email communications. It's exclusive for Kindle readers, and it's where I share my most advanced information.

https://servenomaster.com/NetworkingInvite

If you are reading on a Kindle, you can just click this link. With other formats, you will have to manually enter the link on your Internet browser.

As a new tribe member you will get:

- Access to advanced networking lessons
- Amazing networking contacts and a support network
- Cutting edge job-hunting tactics and strategies

Do you know the big differences between struggling students and successful, masterless entrepreneurs? The truly masterless have a support network that knows them, knows their situation, and treats them like part of a community.

If you've ever wished that someone would give you a hand and give you the social connections that you can already see are so important to success...

Here's your chance, and the barrier is as low as it will ever get.

https://servenomaster.com/NetworkingInvite

Click here and say hello to us today!

PART I
LAY THE GROUNDWORK

DREAM JOB INTERVIEW

At twenty-nine years old, fresh off my master's course, I sent a blind email to every junior college, state school and university near my hometown. Everyone on my course told me that no university or tertiary institution would hire someone who only had a master's degree – you would need a doctorate if you wanted to teach at the collegiate level, so the best I could hope for was a nice private high school job. Everyone on my course – the other twenty-nine people who were older and more experienced than me – went back to similar jobs to the ones they had before starting the master's program with me. They came in as high school teachers and went back to being high school teachers, except for a slight raise and improvement in education.

I wanted more from life. I sent out cold emails and used my networking skills, and eventually I got a meeting with the head of my dream department – all from my networking skills. Sitting in that office, everything I ever dreamed of was waiting for me – everything I had hoped for was possible, as long as I could say the right words in the right order and bring my networking home.

PROACTIVE NOT REACTIVE

$\mathcal{M}$ost of us are very passive job seekers and we don't even realize it. We only react to what's out there when looking for a job – we only apply to companies who post openings and we only respond to what we see. We never go out and create our own jobs, and that's a limitation.

When your dream company posts your dream job, everyone sees it at the same time. That changes the game – you are competing with every other person who has the same dream job as you. If you are not new to the job market, you probably know that things are getting very crowded at the moment.

A lot of really big companies have recently been run into the ground by poor executive leadership. Tens of thousands of people who are far more qualified than me have lost their jobs because of decisions outside their control. You can't blame the engineers when the owner of the company makes an acquisition for millions of dollars that turns out to be worthless. In my short lifetime, I have seen this happen dozens of times. It's astonishing to see that despite what they've paid for the acquisition, there is no way to make that money back.

People are still buying and selling Myspace; that website hasn't made money in twenty or thirty years. You can't control what your boss does and that can seriously affect your destiny. There are people in the job market now who are incredibly qualified, and in fact, a lot of those people out there looking for jobs are far more qualified than me.

Despite all of this, I know that every time I enter the market, every time I seek a new position, I have nothing to worry about because they are all doing the same thing – waiting to see a job get posted and then sending out a resume. They are waiting to hear about an opportunity, and only then they react.

If you want to get ahead of the curve, you have to be proactive. That means starting before everyone else. The person who starts their preparation the earliest and prepares the most is always the one who wins.

Most people start looking for a job the day they lose their last one. If you want to be ahead of the curve, you should start weeks, months or even years in advance. You should aim at building a network of contacts, friends, and connections that will be there for you when you need them the most. This is what it means to be proactive, to positively affect your environment.

Waiting until you need a favor to start building relationships is far too late.

SHORTEN THE JOB SEARCH

People add me on LinkedIn all the time. I am a LinkedIn super connector with thousands of contacts, and people link to me trying to expand their job-seeking efforts. When someone adds me and they are unemployed I can tell right away, and it's very different compared to when someone adds me before they need me.

The sooner you start taking action – the sooner you start taking charge of your destiny – the faster you can get back to work and become effective. You can shrink the job-seeking cycle down from months to weeks, to even days or hours. It's not so much what you know – it's who you know. Even in a digital world where everything is handled through technology, Internet and electrons shooting across the stratosphere, human connection is still everything. I do most of my business online; ninety-nine percent of my connections are purely digital.

Still, that human connection, that personal touch means everything.

Make the decision right now to be proactive in your job search. As we go through this guide and this journey together, I'm going to share with you very specific action steps to take.

ACTIVITY

The very first action I would like you to take is to buy a special note-book and a special pen, and maybe even a special backpack – these will form your job-seeker package. In your job-seeking notebook, you will write down your strategies, your plans, and the steps you are going to implement – you will put everything in one place.

I know that the majority of the people who buy this book will buy it digitally, read it on Kindle or maybe listen to it as an audiobook, and only occasionally people will buy the paperback. But you are not going to keep this book with you all the time, and you certainly don't want to show up at a networking event and pull out a book that says "Networking for Job Seekers" – I know that.

Your second action step is therefore to be proactive and start taking notes – start building a strategy saying, "I'm going to be responsible and I'm going to get a great job as soon as possible."

This guide is not about you getting a job like the one you had before. If you are currently out of work, I want your next job to pay more than your last one. That's what this guide is going to teach you how to do. How to make at least ten percent more money each time you change positions –that's the power of effective networking.

AVERAGE EFFORT GETS YOU
AVERAGE RESULTS

*I*f you do the same things as everyone else, you will get the same results as everyone else. If you treat your job seeking casually, you will get casual results. This is what most people do without realizing it. Most people, including people who think they are doing the best thing, are being 'active' by printing out hundreds and even thousands of resumes a day, passing them out door to door and asking for interviews.

Unfortunately, they are still implementing an average strategy. You can put a lot of gas into a broken engine, but it is still not going to make the car go fast. That's what can happen if you have been working this hard – if you have been working ten times harder than everyone else but if you can't figure out how to turn resumes into interviews and interview into jobs – this is where your strategy is starting to falter.

You are putting a lot of energy into a strategy that is not working. The definition of insanity is doing the same thing over and over again, expecting a different result. That is what keeps happening to you. You want a different result and you deserve a different result, but you need a different action in order to get that.

You have taken a great first step. You are reading this book, you are on this journey with me, and I'm going to show you some unconventional tactics that are going to make a difference for you.

Begin by looking beyond the average tactics now. The way to know when a strategy is average is to see if everyone else is doing the same thing.

GO AGAINST THE FLOW

Every year, there are three or four books written by executives of big companies that become a trend. Everyone gets interested in them and everyone starts using the terms found in the latest corporate inspirational book.

I worked at a very large corporation more than ten years ago, and they made everyone watch a presentation based on the book Who Moved My Cheese, which is funny because the book is all about escaping a job you don't like. It was obvious that the people giving the presentation and the people who had decided that everyone in the company needed to watch this presentation did not understand the book. We often hear this new idea, new strategy or a new term that everyone starts using, and almost everyone implements poorly or doesn't understand.

You're not going to get your next job by doing exactly what I did and I am not going to pretend that you are. It's impossible to replicate the exact series of steps that led to that interview and that led to my story.

Pretending that two people can replicate each other's fate – well, that's ridiculous and illogical; we know that life doesn't work that way.

Ask a hundred different married couples how they met and you'll hear a hundred different stories. How many people do you know who met their husband or wife the same way their parent met? Of course not many. So why do we expect that from our professional careers? Why do we suddenly lose our sense of logic and our sense of reality when it comes to job hunting? If you want to be beyond the average, don't get caught up in the trends.

The tactics and strategies in this book are universal. They apply to every area of life. Initially, I didn't learn them as a job seeker – I learned them when I wanted to find love. These strategies are the reason I have a wife and wonderful children.

Understanding social connections and how to meet people is the key. It becomes a cycle. I used my social skills to form a business contact, who introduced me to his business partner, who then asked me to do a social favor and go on a blind double date with him. I tried to resist, but because I was in the middle of a business deal I had no choice. It was the worst date of my life – I tried to leave early by sneaking out of the date and they caught me. So I married her.

This is the power of networking. It's not just about job seeking, but it is a very powerful tactic for job seeking. It will affect and influence every area of your life, but you have to be exceptional – you can't use average effort and you can't use average tactics.

When you do average things, you get average results. It doesn't matter if you are the most qualified person for the position, very rarely is a person hired based purely on their qualifications. If they were, there would be no job interviews – there would be computers doing the hiring.

Most hiring decisions are made by Human Resource Managers who don't fully understand what your job is actually going to entail. There are a lot of rules and steps that they have to implement to do with gender, race and other demographics they have to fill in, in order to stay competitive. All of these complicated and socially-dictated rules demand that companies do far more to make a profit. They have to make a profit, they have to make a difference, they have to help the environment, and they have to be diverse in very specific ways.

These complications are the reason why so many companies set up HR departments just to keep track of all the new laws that the government passes. Federal, state and local government pass tens of thousands of new laws every year. There is literally no human being who can name every law that applies to them.

You can talk to the mayor of every city, and they will not know every law that applies to them. Even if they somehow managed to remember every single municipal law, they won't know all of the state laws and they certainly won't know all of the federal laws.

Sometimes, we pass laws that are meant to help society and make our lives better, but other times we don't delete old and contradictory laws and they begin to make things worse. We are very good at passing laws, but we are very bad at ending and closing them.

This is why you can't be average. The system is rigged against you. It doesn't matter your age, your gender, your sexual orientation, your race – none of that matters anymore. Whatever your situation is, there are laws that are against you.

There are so many laws on the books and so many rules rigged against everyone – no matter what your set of circumstances is. If you think that you're special and this doesn't apply to you, you are caught up in a mindset that is going to slow down your job seeking process.

BINARY DECISIONS

People hire people they like, and that needs to be our focus. You don't need to be a quota hire. You want to be the new employee that people are excited about. Whether you are twenty or seventy, a man or woman, none of that matters. You want everyone to be excited when you show up – you don't want people to groan and think, "Oh, they're just filling the quota." That sucks! I have been on both sides, and it's terrible to feel that way.

I understand accepting a job because you need it, no matter what the circumstances, but all of that only happens if you are not in control. As a true job-seeking networker, you will be in control of every aspect of your job search, which means you will get multiple job offers and you will choose the job you want.

When you have multiple offers at once, you can pick the one that fits you best – the job you are most excited about, the right one for you. How about the one that pays the most money? Or the one that gives you an educational side or will pay for your travel or will give you the most vacation days?

Most people choose a job between job and no job. People end up in bad relationships exactly in the same way – they choose between being single and being with whoever will have them.

What happens to the people on those fancy dating TV shows with their twenty options? Everything changes, they're in total control. Having twenty options for your partner is just as exciting as having twenty options for your job. We are going to create an environment where you have those options.

ACTIVITY

Your goal right now is "To Be Exceptional," and that's what I want you to write in your job-seeker journal. Write down things about you that make you different from everyone else. If you have a degree that's great, but everyone has a degree, everyone has a gender, an age, a race – you want to go beyond that and find what makes you exceptional.

What do you know that other people don't know? What can you do that other people don't know how to do? What are you willing to do to get your dream job that other people aren't willing to do? What strategies are you willing to implement?

Write down a couple of your ideas, but mostly write down, "I am willing to be exceptional," and make that your mantra. You are no longer going to put in average effort and you are no longer going to use average strategies. They don't work and they leave you with the dirty taste of disappointment in your mouth – and let's be honest, you deserve better than that.

MANIPULATE THE BATTLEFIELD

$\mathcal{J}$ do not play fair, and I will never compete with you on even footing. Whatever I can do to manipulate the deck against other job seekers, I will do it. Whatever I can do to manipulate the interview in my favor, I will do it because, at the end of the day, it is my job to make enough money to support my wife and feed my children.

We have this mindset based on fairness and all these rules based on ethics that everyone subscribes to, even though they are not actual ethics. Fairness isn't real, and in this chapter we are going to shatter that mindset.

You can come home to your family and say, "Guys, we have to sell the house and you can't go to school anymore. Even though you're sixteen, you have to get a job at a fast food joint to support the family. Why? Because I went to an interview and I could have gotten the job, but I had to be fair. They asked who would do the job better and I pointed to the other person and said he deserves it more, so he got the job and now my children are hungry."

Is that the fate you want? It's not the fate I want for you and it's certainly not the fate I want for me.

You are reading this book and that means you are part of my tribe now. The name of our tribe is *Serve No Master*. That means it is all about you. I am a mercenary and I don't deny it, I am a capitalist and I don't deny it. If you are looking for a job then you are a capitalist. Jobs are where we exchange work for money.

We're on the same page, so be honest with yourself and be honest about who you are. I am not talking about slashing other people's tires or setting traps here – I am talking about manipulating the social battlefield.

For example, imagine you go for a job interview and as you are about to shake hands with the HR manager, the CEO of the company walks by and says to you, "Hey Sally! Oh, you are interviewing today? I am so glad you are here; I hope things go well for you in there. Good luck, I would love to have you on the team," and then walks away.

The HR manager sees that, and even though there are ten other people waiting, suddenly your interview is first. Do you think that the odds have been stacked in your favor? Yes. Have you done anything unethical? No. All you did was use your networking skills to build a relationship before the job interview.

THE ONLY APPLICANT

Companies usually go through several phases when looking to fill a position. First, they look internally to see if there is anyone already within the company they can grow into the position. When that happens, a different position opens up and they keep shifting people around until they find a position they can't fill internally.

Then they go into phase two, where the company will announce, "Hey, we've got this position open and we are looking for someone. Do you know someone who would be good?" The send this email around the company hoping to get a great internal recommendation.

Some companies even pay a bounty. When you work at company X and you find a new candidate and bring them in, if they are the right fit and the person is hired, you can get paid a bounty. This is how the entire headhunting industry exists. Headhunters bringing in C-level candidates, accountants or high-level managers get paid a massive commission if their candidate gets hired. That only happens in phase three and four; phase two is internal, so only the people working within the company know about it. This means that if you want to work for a company and you know everyone who works there, they will put you forward for every job that comes up. You will get the job interview and there won't be any competition.

In round one, they only interview people who work at the company. In round two, they only interview people that get recommended by current employees. Instead of being in the room with ten, twenty or thirty people, waiting your turn, in round two you are the only one there because someone recommended you.

The person who recommended you will be tip the odds of getting the job in your favor, and you can manipulate this process so that not just one person but ten or twenty will put your name in. Do you think HR is going to look on you favorably when you show up after twenty different people have said you are the perfect person for the job?

They are going to give you that job, as long as you don't lose it by acting crazy in the interview. I have walked into job interviews where they have literally handed me a schedule. I go, "I thought this was a job interview." They go, "You are already hired." That is the power of manipulating the battlefield; it comes from a willingness to use unconventional tactics.

When I say manipulating the battlefield, I mean being the first if not the only person to be interviewed. This is how you can land a job before anyone else knows about it.

HIRING PHASES

There is a process to posting jobs online. Here is how it works: A company realizes they need to fill a position; this can happen in a myriad of ways – someone quits, someone gets fired, the company is growing and they have an opening, someone gets shifted, or someone gets pregnant and takes maternity leave. The company realizes this position needs to be filled.

Depending on the size of the company, a department will send a message to HR, "Hey, we need this position filled. Here are the job specs." In larger companies, every position has a sheet detailing the job description, the job requirements, what the person will do and what the expectations are. They shoot this information over to HR and the person in HR begins to add it to their information network.

First, they may add it to the company's website, if the company has a vacancies list. Second, they will go through the process of adding it to the different websites where they post ads – there are a couple of platforms I am sure you are familiar with, where most jobs get posted. Third, there is a possibility that they will send out a job to their head-hunters' network saying what the position is and what the bounty will be, "Go fill it."

There is a first window of opportunity, when the initial message goes to HR, when it is decided that, "We need to hire someone," before it goes public over the wire. That period of time can be anywhere from a few days to a few weeks.

Companies don't move fast. Even for me, I am a one-man operation, I hire a lot of employees and I have shifted now to doing more long-term contracts. I have employees from all around the world who help me with my business. (I hire them through different websites and I will post links on my Networking for Job Seekers page for you.)

But even for me, when I am thinking of hiring someone, I go through a period of time where I start talking to people around me. I hired a social media manager just last month, and this came about because someone in my social circle was interested in the position and I said, "Do you know what? I am actually looking to hire someone." She got the opportunity to get the job before I posted it.

Unfortunately, this particular person missed her chance. She missed a few communication moments and I got very nervous. I'm not big on talking every day, but I do want to be able to reach the people who work for me. If I send you a message and don't get an email back for a week, I am not comfortable with that – especially since I pay every week. I don't want to have to pay to not have heard from you in a week. After it didn't work out with her, I posted the job opening online.

The larger your social network, the more often the battlefield is tipped in your favor. The more contacts you have, the more likely that one of them will know about a job opening that would be perfect for you. They will know about job openings before the general public finds out and you can use this insider knowledge to get solo interviews. That is the power of manipulating the battlefield.

ACTIVITY

It's time to get a little bit creative now. You are going to crack out your job-seeker notebook and write down a few different ways you can manipulate the battlefield.

What are the advantages you can have? What would the advantage be if you were the only person applying for the position? What would the advantage be if you were the only one submitting an application – the only one to be interviewed that day? How is it different and what is the advantage of doing that when there is no one else around? How is it an advantage to have the CEO be the one to recommend you? What is the advantage of coming in obliquely, manipulating the battlefield?

I want you to think of a few other ideas – I want you to be creative here. Whatever industry you are in, there are different ways you can manipulate the battlefield.

To give you an example, there was this guy who was looking for his dream job. He found every person in his town who was in charge of hiring people for that type of position. He bought ads on Google AdWords and he ran them based on their names, so that whenever someone Googled their own name, an ad would pop up saying, "Hey Jason, I would love to work for you." It was so dynamic and so creative that the guy got interviewed by all the different people he ran ads on and he got his dream job. The total cost if his idea? Less than five dollars to get himself a nice seven-figure payday. That's a pretty nice turnaround on just posting some ads.

Get to working on your own ideas, get creative and spend some real time with your notebook. When you finish and are ready, I will be waiting for you in the next section. We are just getting warmed up and I haven't told you all of my ideas. We have a lot more ground to cover.

THREE DEGREES OF SEPARATION

$\mathcal{M}$ost of the business world is built around three degrees of separation. Most great job opportunities come from a friend, a friend of a friend or a friend of a friend of a friend. One, two, three degrees of separation. You are unlikely to get hired by someone you are good friends with. You are unlikely to work directly with someone you are friends with, and in fact, you don't want that – it's too close.

I made that mistake when my business began to grow. Every time I hired one of my friends, it turned into a nightmare. One degree of separation is too close because you have other parts of the relationship. Business and friendship mix up, and that is not ideal because while one of you is making a business decision, the other is making a friendship decision. When you hire someone you are friends with, eventually you will have to make a decision about firing them or giving them a raise. It can become a complicated situation, and you want to avoid that nightmare.

Many studies show that most great jobs and great hirings don't come from too far away either. Strangers don't get hired as much as soft acquaintances. What we really want to do is build out our network, and this is the science behind LinkedIn. This is not a book advertising LinkedIn – this is a book that simply points out that understanding the three degrees of separation is LinkedIn's brilliance.

The guy who built LinkedIn based his algorithm on the three degrees of separation principle. He exchanged his algorithm for owning a percentage of Facebook, and now just that part of Facebook is worth far more than LinkedIn as a whole. This one simple concept can define how we form business alliances, romantic relationships, and friendships.

You don't work with friends and you don't want to work with strangers. You want to work with someone who is a little bit vouched, so that you know they are OK to work with, but not someone so close to you that you can't fire them, fight with them or be strict with them. That's the balance we find in the three degrees of separation – a little bit of distance, a friend of a friend or a friend of a friend of a friend – one, two, three. This is why it is so critical to expand your network, the number of people you know, and the number and type of people you orbit.

The average job seeker is a very good technical worker. I have a friend who is one of the biggest helpers for job seekers in the world. He has helped thousands of people get back to work by helping them build out LinkedIn profiles. He was even gracious enough to write the foreword at the start of this book.

I have been friends with him for a long time; he mentored me in building my business and during that time I helped him we worked on a lot of resumes together. I was astounded – almost every person who was looking for a job had a resume that made me look like common street trash. I would be helping people with their resume and be thinking that person was ten times smarter than me; they were an expert at the hard sciences but they failed at the soft sciences. They knew everything they needed to do their job, but nothing about how to get a promotion, form a connection, or get a new position – something always fell through.

THE SOFT SCIENCES

The story at the beginning of this book starts with me sitting in front of the head of my dream department applying to be an administrator. It wasn't just to be a teacher; I was also going to be in charge of six other teachers.

I can only describe myself as horribly under-qualified for the position. I had never managed anyone before and had no idea how to do that. Every other person in the department was older and more experienced than me. They were all masters of their craft, but I had focused on the soft sciences and that's why the opportunity came to be in front of me.

> We spend so long focusing on being good at our jobs that we forget how important it is to build relationships.

People want to work with people they like, people want to give promotions to people they like. Being unknown is nearly as bad as being disliked.

When the boss is handing out bonuses and someone goes, "Hey, we should give Thomas a bonus." And the boss goes, "Thomas who?" "Thomas, he's the guy that works really hard." Maybe Thomas works really hard but he is not really memorable. We don't want to be the forgotten one; we don't want to be the one who doesn't count because the boss forgot you exist. This happens to people, especially now that more and more jobs require a great deal of technical work.

You can become the best implementer in the world and you still have to wait for people to notice how great you are. That takes a lot longer. It is better to shorten the cycle so you can get those better jobs and bigger contracts more quickly. This is why we want to focus on growing our networks – that's the value.

Most people get hired based on the network around them. Websites that are called social networks are just a digital example – easy to understand examples of real-life social circles made of our friends, our friends' friends and then our soft acquaintances.

There is an easy way to measure your social circle: how many birthday parties do you get invited to per year? If you get invited to two birthday parties, that is the size of your closest network.

At each party you will meet all the friends you have in common with the birthday person and then you'll meet a circle around them of people you don't really know that well. Sometimes, if the birthday party is at a bar or restaurant, there may be people there that are strangers to you, but they may know you because they are regulars there. These are your three degrees of social circle.

BIRTHDAY PARTIES

Most people have an average of five to seven people in their closest, tightest circle. The next circle around it might be up to twenty people and then the third circle may be two hundred people. This is in real life as opposed to digital life – we will talk about digital life in a bit.

Let's start with face to face, touching life, real life, breathing life before we get into digital tactics.

If you get invited to two birthday parties a year, the odds of getting a job are a two on our "odds-of-getting-hired" scale. If the person you are competing with gets invited to a birthday party every week, their odds are fifty-two – they are twenty-five times more likely to get a job than you. For every job you get offered, they will get offered twenty-five. That's how powerful networking is.

You might be thinking, "Oh my goodness, this guy Jonathan is saying I have to become popular – getting a job is a popularity contest." Not quite! Don't worry. When I was in high school, I was painfully unpopular. I didn't make my first friend in life until I was seventeen, so please believe me when I say I know what it is like to be not liked; what it's like to be despised.

When I was younger – ten, twelve, fifteen – I used to break down and cry because no one liked me. I used to go to schools and summer camps where kids would mostly discuss different ways of killing me. Blowing me up, setting me on fire, hitting me with a nuclear bomb.

You can't do that anymore nowadays – bullying is taken a little bit more seriously – but back then teachers were like, "That's kids being kids." It was a horrible experience for me and on top of that I got ditched at not one but two different proms – both of my dates left me, abandoned me for other guys and shattered my heart against the rocks.

I don't like popularity contests because I know what it's like to be unpopular. But remember what I told you; I don't play fair. You don't have to be cool, you just have to make other people think you are cool, and that is way easier.

ACTIVITY

For this activity, I would like you to study your real social network and measure if your social network is real. Look at your friends in real life – how many people have you eaten a meal with, face to face, in the last three months? Out of those people, if any of them asked your help on finding a job, who would you help? That is the measure of your relationship. If you would help them, then they would help you. If you wouldn't help them, then they wouldn't help you.

It is possible that your number is zero, and that is ok. We can still work with that – at least we know where we are starting.

Most of my relationships are digital. I live on a tropical island, I don't have a lot of face-to-face meals and I don't like having meals with other people. Especially because I have kids and like everyone's kids, they are monsters in restaurants. As a child, my sister was always under the table, and my daughter is just the same. My son's antics at home are hilarious, but when we are out in public or in a restaurant, I don't find them as funny. Even before my kids came into the scene, I never had a lot of group meals. If you aren't much of a meal person, we are going to look at other ways to measure your social network.

Let's look at of your friends on Facebook, LinkedIn, Twitter or whatever social network you want. Of all the people on there, how many have you talked to in a meaningful way in the last year? A meaningful way means you told them something that you didn't post in a public thread. You told them a personal story of any kind, you told them something that you would not post in real life, because we all post birthday messages and our political opinions or our favorite meme or cartoon, but those don't mean anything.

Did you tell one of your friends when you were sick or when you were thinking about quitting your job? Did you tell them one of your hopes and dreams or vice versa? That's how you can define a real connection. Did you talk to someone about what you were thinking of naming your next child or whether you wanted a boy or a girl? These are all meaningful conversations that define our social network.

For most people, the group you had a meal with represents your inner circle, your closer circle. But some of us are purely digital, our online group is our inner circle, and that is okay – we can network in either way, we can do other things. To really build certain things, you need to assess. LinkedIn is pretty cool because it tells you how many friends you have in each circle.

One thing you want to check for as you are self-analyzing is a "closed network". Imagine a hundred people who are all friends with ninety-nine other people, but it is all the same ninety-nine other people. You go, "Wow, I've got ninety-nine people in my first degree of separation!" But then you look at the second level and it's a hard zero. Everyone you know knows each other and you don't know anyone who knows people outside your circle.

This is very common. I know some single people and all their friends are married and they go, "How come I never meet anyone single?" If you look at their circle of friends, it's a closed set. They are the only single person that any of their friends know. You might not notice it, but if you are in a closed set, it's game over. There is no chance of you meeting someone else because no one knows anyone else, even if you go to a thousand parties.

You also want to check to see if your circles are healthy. LinkedIn is pretty cool about this, it shows you first, second and third-degree connections and it will show you your numbers. LinkedIn is not really real, because most of your connections aren't real – they know LinkedIn is about building a large network. You see people who don't have a profile picture, they have twelve friends and their profile is not getting viewed.

You are allowed to have over thirty thousand personal connections on LinkedIn before you have to ask for more. If you ask for more, they will give you another five thousand. So if you have seven, or two hundred, it is nothing. Your large circle, your final circle, should be tens of millions and ideally hundreds of millions of connections – that's when you have a large and powerful network on this digital platform.

ANOTHER ACTIVITY

You want to really look at your current assets. We have looked at what makes you special and now I want you to take some time with your special job-seeker journal and analyze your current social network. What assets do you have? Give yourself a score. "My current social network is awesome." Or, "My current social network is abysmal."

Give yourself an A whether it's good or bad; A, AA, AAA. My current social network is average; my current social network is adequate. You can write down an A and no one else will know that you are giving yourself a terrible score because we only have A words across the spectrum. No one else is going to see this. This is for you because we are going to take your current social network and we are going to set it on fire – we are going to take it to the next level.

It is impossible to measure your success unless you know where you are starting. How can you know how far you have run unless you know where the race started?

We are going to do some amazing things, so assess your social network and be honest with yourself as you work through this activity. Once you have looked at your real life friends, your social network friends, your friends of friends and have really assessed everything, meet me in the next section.

ONLINE AND OFFLINE

We have already begun to hint and talk about online and offline social networks. The ways we use them to network in real life and online are very different.

In preparation for this new book, I recently launched what I called a "LinkedIn Push", where I added a bunch of super-connectors to my network. I basically went proactive again and I wanted to give a new push – I hadn't pushed online on LinkedIn in a long time. I wanted to expand my network again and see how things are going.

I wanted to find out what people do when I invite them into my network. I am very interested in the first messages people send me. I would describe ninety-nine percent of the first messages people send me as tacky, uncouth or gross.

"Hey, watch this video. I want you to see something!"

"Hey, why don't you check out my website?"

"Hey, maybe I can work for you or maybe you know someone who wants to hire me?"

"Hey, I see you have one of the best-selling books on Amazon. You probably don't know how to build a business, why don't you pay me huge amounts of money and I'll build a course for you?"

It's very obvious that many of these are copy and paste or automated messages that have no meaning. They are things you wouldn't say to someone in real life, because it would be so obvious. Would you walk up to someone in real life and read a business card to them? No. But we do it online – we act online in a way that we would never do in person, and we don't even realize it. How about taking the time to read my profile?

Sometimes I mass message too, but you want to be very careful about how you send mass messages. I don't send mass messages on social media. I do send them to people who ask for it. Then I'll say "Hey everyone, I've got a new book coming out," or, "There's something going on in my life," but don't send someone a message until they have asked for it. That is important.

Adding me on LinkedIn is not a license to shove your fist up my bum, trying to force-feed your idea or your business opportunity into me.

WHO COACHES THE COACHES?

There is a new business that I encounter all the time and I find it fascinating. It's people who coach coaches, who coach coaches. The last time I was networking in person, I was in California for an event (I only travel twice a year, once a year to California and once a year to Thailand, for to two very large networking events).

I was walking to person after person who said, "Oh, I coach coaches". Then I met someone who said, "I coach coaches, who coach coaches." My friends and I couldn't stop laughing – it sounded to us like a pyramid scheme. Maybe some of these people actually do help people, but they never help the end user, and that is the kind of business I have always struggled to be in.

Yes, in my business I also do some coaching. I teach people to write books and how to become bestsellers. But that's what I do myself – I write books and I always have multiple books on the bestseller books list on Amazon. I teach people to do what I am doing.

When you are trying to teach people to do something that you are not actually doing, well it's hard for me to take that very seriously.

What is the proof that what you do works? You don't even know how to do it. If I want to learn how to fight, I want to learn from the guy who has been punched in the face. I don't want to learn from the guy who has read a bunch of books about pain management.

There is a lot to be said for great boxing trainers, and not all of them were great boxers. Being a boxing trainer is not an easy job, there is a great deal of craft to it. If you aren't very good, everyone will know because the first fight your guy is in, he will lose real bad, and then you will never get another job again.

When you are coaching coaches to coach coaches, however, it's hard to know what you are actually doing. "Well, I can't show my client, we all have NDAs and everything is secret, but I'm really good at it and there are huge amounts of money." I get these messages all the time – this happens to be the trend right now.

I get these messages on LinkedIn and I find them ridiculous because they don't mean anything; we haven't even formed a connection yet. This is a very common digital mistake.

People make horrible networking mistakes in person, but I find these mass, empty messages to be quite egregious and a great waste of opportunity.

BUSINESS CARDS

We have the online world and the offline world. The online world is filled with social networks and apps; it is the Internet. And then we have meatspace, or whatever you want to call it – the non-internet; the human world, face-to-face world, where your body dwells while your mind might be online.

In the physical world, you go to events and people pass out business cards like crazy. A business card is basically social trash. Business cards are pretty much the herpes of social interactions. Do you remember in the 90s, when AOL was constantly giving away Compact Disks that came with two free hours, thirty free hours, ninety-nine free hours of Internet?

Those CDs were everywhere – they became ubiquitous. They

were so common I had to learn the word ubiquitous. When I go to an event, that is how I perceive business cards. If you pass out a thousand business cards, one of them will turn into a real connection if you are extremely lucky. If you are a normal person, it will be one out of ten or even a hundred thousand. That's a lot of trees you murdered for one real contact.

A system is ineffective if the ratio is below one out of ten. Really, your ratio should be far higher, but anything below one out of ten is ridiculous and extremely brash. Underlings hand out business cards with a dozen ways to reach them, and bosses hand out business cards that don't have real information on them.

I can't tell you how many times a CEO or a business executive has handed a business card to me and if you call the number on it, their secretary answers. This care really means, "Here's the number to my gatekeeper, I don't want to have a real connection with you."

What has happened is you have formed a connection with a real person, you have talked to the guy for five minutes. Then he said, "Here's my card, give me a call sometime." You call, you talk to the gatekeeper, and she doesn't know you. You thought you would have a warm call, but it's ice-cold because you've phoned a stranger and that is no good – it's not going to convert. People do it all the time. That business card was a step backward in your communication.

People go to events with a thousand business cards and they pass them out, pass them out, pass them out, and then nothing happens but you can't figure it out. If you think of business cards as seeds you're planting, you have to realize that most business cards are terribly designed, terribly ineffective, and they don't go anywhere. I usually come home from events with five or six business cards.

I normally tell everybody I don't take business cards, but some people are adamant that I accept their card. I'll pull their business card out of my bag and go, "I don't remember who this is". What good is that? I don't remember what this person and I talked about. I only want real connections.

THE SHOTGUN APPROACH

I don't try to form a thousand weak connections. I would rather form ten strong connections. As you build each of those ten strong connections, you get access to each of their networks.

> You don't need to build your third degree of separation; you only need to build your first.

If you have a strong inner circle of people you know – people you are willing to talk to when you are looking for someone to be a part of a new project or start a new job – they will put the word out to their network, and that is when you get access to a hundred thousand people instead of a dozen. A few strong connections are worth far more than many soft connections.

As you are networking, whether it is online or offline, you want to be exceptional. You want to be memorable and you don't want to be tacky or obvious. You want to do what everyone else is not doing.

How about this – when someone adds you on LinkedIn, read their profile and say, "Hey, I noticed that you are from Cambridge, Massachusetts. Fascinating! I almost went to Tufts." Or, "My favorite team is the Boston Celtics – I don't know if you are a fan, but I thought that was pretty cool about your profile." That is far better than anything else – it is rapport seeking. You are saying, "Hey, I read your profile and I see you as a human." That is very valuable online. Actually, it covers quite a lot of ground. You will get a much better response rate compared to that mass email you have been sending out to everyone, offering your tax services, a free training video or a free training webinar that everyone knows is a pre-recorded auto webinar – no one is fooled.

People are aware of how the Internet works and can tell when they are watching a pre-recorded video. Start to think that way.

When I meet a new person, when I form a connection, I go for something real. I don't exchange phone numbers very often. Part of the reason for this is because I live internationally and most of my contacts are in different time zones.

When I meet someone, I say, "Hey, give me your Skype," because Skype is my primary source of communication. I don't take emails. I think an email address is one degree better than a business card at best. For some people it is the opposite – emailing is their main form of communication. Not for me.

I check my email once, at the start of my day, and then I don't look at it for the rest of the day. Whereas Skype I leave on all the time, so if you send me a message to my Skype I will see it, it goes to my phone. That's why I don't give Skype to very many people. You only get my Skype if you are a real connection, if we actually connected on a real level and have something to talk about.

CONFETTI

Think about this – it's not only about the information we give out, but that information tells people how you see them. I have done a lot of experiments with business cards and I want to share with you a personal story that may make me sound a little pretentious.

When I first started building my own business in 2010, I began going to local networking events. At this point, I was already a Jedi networker – I was already a level-ten networker and I was one of the youngest people at these events. You can find them at meetup.com.

I really recommend going to them – they are a great place to practice your social networking because you are surrounded by people who are desperate. You don't have to start the conversation – they'll do anything to talk to you.

The first one I went to, someone had already put a business card on each place mat at the bar where we were all meeting. There were business cards already waiting for me and they said, "Hey, you should do the same thing!" A bunch of people had done it. Anywhere you sat, there were already five or six business cards waiting for you – waiting to be tossed straight into the garbage.

Even if one of them seemed a little bit intriguing, I didn't know this person. You wouldn't call those phone numbers in the back of a restroom where it says, "call for a good time," would you? I wouldn't. It's weird and feels like a trap.

If I called the number on one of these bathroom business cards, I probably wouldn't meet the person pictured on it – it would be someone totally different. If I called this number, they'd probably meet me at the hotel, murder me and steal my kidney. That's what I expect to happen – there is no trust. With no rapport and no trust, with no connection, a business card has no more value than a number scrawled on a bathroom wall.

When I was at one of these events, I caught the lay of the land and I thought I needed a business card. I made one that had ten digits on it – it had my cell phone number and nothing else. I would only give it to someone once we had formed a connection. I'd start talking to someone and they'd hand me their business card right at the beginning of the conversation. I'd go, "Oh, I haven't met you yet," and they'd go, "Where's your business card?" I'd then say that I only give it to people that I talk to – I don't give my card to strangers because my time is very valuable.

Eventually, after a bit of conversation, I might give someone my card and they'd say, "But your name isn't on here!" Then I would say, "If you don't remember my name, please don't call me."

I know it sounds pretentious, and it is. As a kid, I was a big fan of watching the X-Files and I am pretty sure I got this from that TV show. I just remember there was a CIA agent – a spy who just had a phone number and no name. I thought it was cool and I tried it in the business world. It actually sends a very clear message.

That number it goes straight to my cell phone, not to an assistant and then to my office, so no one called if they couldn't remember my name. And guess what, all you need is a pen – you can write my name on the card. It's made out of paper!

I was encouraging people to be smart. I encouraged people to write my name, what they remembered about me, and the reason they would want to call me on the card. I was encouraging them to network better. Then the card would become valuable, because in reality we mostly keep cards just in case, "Maybe someday I'll call this person."

There are certain types of cards that we'll always need at some point – a mechanic, a plumber, an electrician, a hair stylist. These are all generally useful contacts because at some point in life you'll have a problem and this is the person you will need to call. The rest of the time it's like, "Oh well, just in case I need someone who is a coach, or who coaches coaches."

I did meet someone similar, but he called himself a "business architect". I said, "Oh, you're an architect," and he said, "Yeah, I help businesses design their future." My brother in law is an architect and he designs buildings. That is what an architect actually is, if you rely on the dictionary, but these days people think if they make up a job that no one has ever heard of before they will get more business. I don't know if it works, but I didn't take him seriously after seeing that card.

NOT ENOUGH TIME

Going back to my cards with no name, very rarely would people call me. But when they did, the contacts were very valuable. Everyone who met me thought I was very successful; I created the mystique of success before I had created success. I acted like a successful person; I acted like my time was valuable – because it is.

Imagine for a second that you hand out a thousand business cards and everyone calls you. You know that there is no value to a relationship with most of the people you handed out your business cards to. Imagine each person calls you and they each want to talk to you for ten minutes – just to find out about your life and your family. Just a friendly conversation.

They aren't doing anything wrong – in fact, they are doing something very sweet. It would be nice if people were actually like this in our society.

But with a thousand people asking for ten minutes of your time, that is ten thousand minutes. If you do a little math, that is a lot of time. Every six people takes an hour, every sixty people takes ten hours of your life. Six hundred people is a thousand hours, and the math can go on and on. But the point is that it's a lot of wasted time and all leading to nothing. If you had all those conversations, all you would have is a mild connection with a thousand people that would never lead anywhere.

It would take you an entire week of talking on the phone to maintain those relationships. That week you would have no time for eating, going to the bathroom or sleeping. When we hand out so many cards that we could never maintain those relationships, we are acting like the relationship won't continue. We are treating the cards as worthless.

What we want to focus on again is the three degrees of separation theory. People don't hire first degrees of separation. No one is going to go, "Hey, I got your business card, we talked for ten minutes and I want to hire you." What they will say is, "Hey, my friend Sam said you were pretty cool so I thought I would give you a call." That is how you get hired and that is the kind of network you want to build, whether it is online or offline.

We are going to build both kinds of networks together. I do suggest starting to expand your LinkedIn network, because that is a network that is built around job seeking and it will get you viewed by more headhunters and HR reps. You also want to build your in-person network, which means going out to events, meeting people, and forming connections. You need to take both steps.

ACTIVITY

It's time to crack out your job-seeker notebook. You are going to write down some ideas and some steps that we are going to take together. Please make the following commitments and write them down.

#1 I am going to form more connections on LinkedIn.

#2 I am going to make my LinkedIn profile perfect.

Most people have garbage pictures, and I am being very generous when I use the word "garbage" there. I have seen pictures that looked like they were taken a hundred years ago. I don't know how they found a camera with such low resolution. I have also seen pictures where the person looks terrible or it is obvious that other people have been cropped out. You have to be serious about your profile picture.

#3 I am going to finish off the rest of my profile.

Take a lot of time to write out your resume. Write out all of the things that make you excellent. Write out all of the things that make you interesting – all of the places you have worked, where you went to school. Join a bunch of groups that are relevant to you. Make it a proactive profile.

#4 I am going to work on my real life network.

Begin attending networking events in real life. You don't have to be proactive just yet. As we go through other chapters, we are going to get more and more active, but for now I just want you to go out and see how people network.

Head over to meetup.com – it always has events listed, no matter how small your town is. Find an entrepreneurs' meetup or a small business owners' meetup. You don't have to go to one for your industry yet. What you want to see is how people who are desperate for networking network.

You can also look in your area for small events – there are always networking events, job seeking events, and job seeker fairs. Go to one of these not as a job seeker, but simply as a person who is observing.

If anyone asks if you are looking for a job, you can say, "I'm just checking out the lay of the land. I like meeting new people and going out, and this seemed like an interesting event. I always keep my ear to the ground and listen to those old railroad tracks to see what's coming around the bend, and I am always looking for cool opportunities."

I want you to write down that phrase in your own language – write it down however you speak. Maybe you'll say "really interesting opportunities" or "really exciting opportunities". What this says is, "I'm not desperate for a job, but if something worthy of my time comes up, I'll take it."

This is more advanced networking, and I want you to memorize this as your own phrase. The idea is that instead of saying you are looking for a job, you are saying, "If you've got one and it's good enough, I might take it." This will get you offered a little more money when you do get offered a job. That's how you get offered a hundred and twenty thousand dollars a year instead of a hundred and five. They will think, "This person is a little bit more elite than what we are looking for."

When you are not looking for a job, they've got to convince you it's worth taking. You are increasing your perceived value. I want you to look online and find several events you are going to go to in the next two weeks. Please go to at least one event, but ideally you should go to three.

Only at live events can you find out how people act. Observe what people do. Use the information I have already given you to analyze their efforts. Pay attention to how people express their need for a job, hand out business cards and interact with each other.

Do they act like normal people? Do people actually want to be your friends or do they act like they are looking for something from you?

When you go to a networking event and you are the one person who is not desperate, you start to feel like the only woman in a bar full of wolves. You'll be a pretty girl in a bar with five hundred guys all desperate for your attention. Once you see bad networking, it will be much easier for you to understand, master, and implement good networking.

PART II
SEVEN SECRETS

THE OTHER SIDE

You've done it – you've made it through the first half of the book, and theory time is over! We have talked about a lot of ideas and concepts, and hopefully you have done your homework. At the very least, at the end of the chapter you found and wrote down a couple of events you can go to, but ideally you have already been to those events and now you are ready for this section. Get ready to go beyond ideas and beyond observing – get ready for the nitty-gritty action time.

STEP ONE: FOCUS ON DECISION MAKERS

$\mathcal{W}$hen we are networking, we choose who to spend time with, and this decision is more important than any other step. I own my business. When I go to events with five thousand people and talk to the people at the early stages of starting their own businesses, I can spend time and invest in those relationships but I will get no return on them. They are all way earlier in their business cycle than me. None of them is hiring people, none of them is expanding their audience yet – they are at the beginning.

I need to find people who are at my level or above. I need to network and connect with other business owners who can share an audience with me, who can share ideas with me – this is where I can expand and build my business.

The same thing applies to you. You want to network with shot callers. You want to network with the CEO, not the guy in the mailroom. The power you hold comes from your introduction, and the person who introduces you determines your worth.

If the mailman introduces you to the CEO, the CEO might give you two or three minutes of their time because he will think you are just another mailman. If the CEO introduces you to the mailroom guy, however, he will think you know the CEO and you get the absorbed perception – this magical and wonderful passed-on power. You want to form your first circle of degree of separation with people who have power.

We have talked a bit about white-collar jobs, but let's talk about blue-collar. Imagine that you work in a factory and you want to get a job in a better factory. You don't want to target other guys who work on the same floor as you, you want to target managers and bosses. You want to form a network with people who have the ability to override HR and say, "Hey HR, I don't care, give her the job. I like her, she's got moxy." I don't think anyone uses that word anymore, but I like it – it means a bit of panache, a bit of excitement and determination, force of character.

You want to surround yourself with people who can give you the maximum bang for your buck. Again, we circle back to some of the earlier principles of manipulating the battlefield.

If you can form a relationship with just one person at the company, why not the person who has the most value? Why not the person who has the most to offer to you? Your first step, your first strategy, is to focus on who you are going to target. You want to know what you want from life – where you want to take your business and your career. That will help you with the rest of this process.

ACTIVITY

Before we go onto step two, write out exactly who your target is.

Who are the right people for you? Do you need to meet HR managers? Do you need to meet bosses? Do you need to meet a specific type of person? Think about the ideal social network for you. If you had ten new, perfect people added to your life, who would they be?

Maybe for your profession it doesn't need to be CEOs, maybe it needs to be the head of a certain department. The head of sales might be more valuable to you as a connection than the CEO or the head of IT – that's ok.

We want to go from the general to the specific; we want to build a strategy that works for you. Write down in your job-seeker journal the people you want to pull into your circle. Knowing your target, we can then build the rest of your strategy.

I was watching a TV show about soldiers recently. Someone was being held hostage and they couldn't rescue the hostages, until the soldiers knew where they were. It's the same principle – you can't build out a rescue mission, you can't work out a plan, until you know who you are dealing with.

I want you to sit down and be real serious; this is a conversation I have with high-level networkers all the time. I have a friend who is one of the best networkers in the world – one of the few people who are better than me. He said to me, "Who is the perfect person for me to introduce you to? What is the ideal connection for you, for me to look for?"

The answer to that question has changed a little bit for me, and I will open up with you. For a while, I was looking for a lot of ghost-writing jobs but I have recently had some problems with my eyes. I got exhausted of writing books for other people and I shifted from taking a lot of ghostwriting jobs to taking only the occasional job.

Right now, I am only ghostwriting for people that are very inter-esting – interesting stories I want to be a part of and I am excited by; books I would want to put my name on. Maybe someone on televi-sion, a rock star, a moderately notorious criminal – maybe a jewel thief more than a murderer. Something that is really interesting basically.

If you ask me what I'm looking for, I'll say I'm looking for people who are looking for coaching, or for me to help them through the process of launching their book. That to me is really interesting right now – helping people to write their book and go through the process of becoming a best-selling author on Amazon.

But I am going to be honest with you – my answer changes all the time. Two weeks ago, I would've said I needed to be introduced to a transcriptionist, but now I have already hired someone full-time. I dictate my books because of the problems with my eyes, and she writes my words for me. Every single word that you read went through someone else's hands.

What is your answer to that question?

Write it down.

Who is the perfect person for me to introduce you to right now? If you and I got on the phone and I said I am going to open up my network to you, I'm going to crack out the old Rolodex, who do you want to talk to?

STEP TWO: INTERSECTIONS OF
POWER

$\mathcal{I}$n step one, we isolated your ideal target, the person you want to meet. What we want to do now is get a little more general. Let's say you are a very good dental assistant or hygienist and you work at a dental office; the ideal person for you to meet would be a dentist.

Or if you want to work in a hospital type of environment, something larger than a dental studio, you need to meet a hospital executive. For our example, let's say you want to meet a dentist. You have to figure out: where do dentists hang out? What do dentists have in common? Where do dentists' lives intersect?

I chose dentists because even though I have done this activity before, I have never done it with dentists. This is pushing me a lot out of my comfort zone – I have to come up with this idea in the moment. If you listened to the tapes (the original dictation of this book), you would hear me as I think through this process.

First of all, dentists have conferences, societies, and clubs – that is where I would begin to do my research. When and where do dentists have events? I happen to know a couple of dentists, so I would ask them. If I didn't have any dentists in my social network, I would go onto LinkedIn and look for dentists' networking events or a national dentists' conference – I am sure they have one, or at least they will have a union, group or society. I would look for those first.

Then I would look for local meetup groups for dentists or medical professionals. It's okay to meet a bunch of doctors, because they all probably know dentists and vice versa; if you meet people that are one or two degrees away, it's ok. We're trying to work our way closer.

Sometimes we can't meet people who are our target but at least we've met someone one step away. Maybe there is no dentists' meetup but there is a dental secretaries' meetup and that is OK – those are gatekeepers, just one degree of separation away. These meetups can be online or in person, and they are all worth going to.

Sometimes the scenario can be even easier, like dentists hanging out at a certain country club or restaurant. By doing some research, you can usually find out the types of places where certain types of people or people with certain types of income brackets hang out.

People who make similar amounts of money all go to similar types of restaurants. People who make a hundred thousand dollars a year go to the same band of restaurants; people who make eight thousand dollars a year go to a different band of restaurants. You can choose locations this way.

Right now we are just getting started on the ideas or research phase, and depending on what your strategy is, we will implement different actions based on what we find out.

Just to give you another example, if you wanted to meet celebrities, you could go to restaurants where they usually have dinner (they are pretty expensive though). You can try to go to celebrity-owned clubs (very expensive too) or you can hang out at a coffee shop across the street from an agency. Every celebrity has an agent, and they all go to the agent's offices to talk about movie scripts and plans or to look at presentations. They often want to have a coffee afterward, or maybe there's a juice bar nearby and they'll go grab a juice – we can think about intersections this way.

Whatever industry you're in, or whatever strategy we need to implement, we know who we are looking for. Now we want to start thinking about where we can meet the biggest amount of people in the smallest amount of time. What we are working on here is efficiency.

I don't want you to go to ten places and put in ten batches of effort in order to meet ten dentists. Why not do it all in one place? You can use the same strategy, but if you are more effective you can meet a hundred dentists instead of ten. This is why we focus on places that intersect. Remember we don't want to use average strategy and average implementation.

Be smart and work smarter, not harder. I go to two networking events per year – that is it! I get more networking done in six days than most people do in a hundred.

I live on an island where there is not a single person I could do business with. I could talk to every single person and none of them could affect my career. They are all in totally different industries than mine; most of them don't even speak the same language as me. I am only able to network when I go to these two events, so I have to be supremely efficient. That is why I chose the events that offer the most bang for my buck.

ACTIVITY

For this activity, find and write down some of the places where these people intersect. Some of your answers will be guesses, and that is OK because from guesses we can research and find out if you are right.

If you are more serious about your job or about finding a job, what you will do right now is click on meetup.com, LinkedIn.com, go onto Facebook and look for groups or societies and places where these people hang out.

Check the local newspaper and society pages; look for charity events that these people would go to. "Hey look, there is an event for a dental charity next month. Do you think there will be a lot of dentists at that?" There sure will be!

Being creative separates us from the crowd. Why do you want to go sit through a bunch of interviews when you can go to an awesome gala party, where you can wear a tuxedo or your favorite ball gown and meet a hundred dentists in a single night and plant a hundred seeds?

STEP THREE: FAMILIARITY BREEDS TRUST

"*I* feel like I know you from somewhere. I feel like I've seen you before."

When I hear that phrase, I know I'm in. It's someone's way of saying, "I've seen you a couple of times; I don't know where, but I trust you." Our brains are designed to trust people we have seen repeated times.

If I want to dominate a social venue – become the most popular person in a particular place – if I want a particular person to like me, I go where that person goes all the time and I just happen to be there. I don't talk to them, but I do things so they can see me.

Once someone has seen me five or even up to ten times in a row, they will feel an obligation to talk to me, "Oh, I see you all the time." You can do the same thing and it is no longer you approaching a stranger with something awkward.

You can walk up to that dentist we talked about in the last chapter and say, "I feel like I have seen you at this coffee shop a dozen times," and they'll go, "I thought the same thing!" And you go, "First I thought we went to high school together, but then I realized we just love the same coffee at the same time." Do you see how much easier it is to start a conversation that way? It is very casual and it's not a hard start – it is a soft start.

We have already mentioned the power of introductions: when a person introduces you to someone, that person's level is the level you enter the social circle – that is the power you are given.

In the coffee shop scenario, if the person behind the counter introduces you, you have the authority of the barista; if the manager introduces you, you get a little bit more, and if the owner introduces you, you get the most. There is value in that, but there is also additional value in familiarity. If people see you enough times, they assume they know you. This is atavistic programming – it goes back to tribal days, so you can recognize that someone is on your tribe or team.

Imagine playing an ancient game of lacrosse, where they used to play to the death. You certainly would want to remember who is on your team! You're going to have the people who you are friends with, but out of a team of twenty of thirty people you don't really know everyone – you might not even know everyone's name, but you certainly want to be able to recognize everyone. You want an instant response of familiarity.

This is why if someone goes to school with you and then they change schools and are on the other team, occasionally you will accidentally pass the ball to them because they look familiar. That programming takes over, and we want to take advantage of that because we want to manipulate the battlefield – you don't want to play fair.

If you find a location where you can have your target see you all the time, then you can use that effect. But if it is an event you are at for only two or three days, in that case we can only use the power of the introduction. These are two different tools that we can use.

If you want to become the most popular person in a place, if you want to use the location to your advantage, going there a lot is a big win. You can't just be there though – you have to be a little bit noticeable, so you can't just sit in a corner where no one can see you, you can't wear a disguise, that won't get you any benefits.

I have had people walk up to me and say, "I have seen you before. I don't know why, but let's do business together." I was at an event in California – it was a big party, they had rented a bar and I was talking to everybody. A guy walked up to me and I noticed I knew him from somewhere.

It took us two hours to remember that two years before we had had one of the funniest nights of my life, drinking and partying in the lobby of the hotel we were staying at. We almost did a business deal together but as things do, we got halfway down the page and we diverged.

Not every business deal you make on a drunken night of an event comes true, but many do. It was really exciting; we hugged and I think we took some pictures together. All of that is really wonderful, all of that is really valuable – that is where the goal is.

If you are familiar, you've got a shot. This can really work, and even if you just happen to look like someone they know, people will give you the benefit of the doubt.

ACTIVITY

In your job-seeker journal, write this down:

"I need to go to this place multiple times; I have chosen the right event or the right venues where I need to get noticed."

Your first action step is to practice building familiarity. We want to test that these are the right venues before we put in a ton of effort, and you can only really find out by actually going there.

We don't need to start on our full frontal assault just yet. In the next section, I am going to cover how to be really tactical and strategic. Let's say you found a dental group meetup, you don't need to go to the meetup itself. You know where they are meeting, and you know they go to the same restaurant every week or once a month.

You can just be someone who goes to that restaurant all the time. They will just see you in the restaurant – you are not part of the group yet, you are building familiarity. You are planting a few seeds by them seeing you over and over again. This is one of the ways you can implement this strategy.

In your journal, write down different ways you can begin to breed familiarity – places you can go or things you can do so people see you all the time. Let's build a little strategy.

STEP FOUR: HOW TO DOMINATE ANY
VENUE

*Y*ou can become the most popular and important person in any location, and it is incredibly easy to do. Choose your target venue or location first. If you've already done it, you're already halfway there.

Start by becoming familiar with the staff. Imagine it's a fixed location – conferences are a little different, we'll talk about singular events in a moment – imagine going to the same place over and over again, seeing the same kind of people. You find out the dentists you want to meet always go to this restaurant.

You don't just want to go there on dentists' night; you also want to go there at times when the place is empty. Talk to everyone who works there, and everyone you meet, treat with respect. Say to the bathroom attendant, "Hi, my name is Jonathan, what's your name? Where are you from? What is it like working in here? Tell me one of your craziest stories."

I like to find out someone's name and one fact about them. Here's one of my most common stories: I have a friend who started out as a loose acquaintance. He is a master businessman and also happens to be an amateur archeologist. I ran into him a few weeks ago and I asked him about it again – I haven't seen him in two years and I was excited because he was my main example. He's still on the hunt. This time we ended up sharing a few stories about our kids, but I did bring up the archeology thing. That is my fact about him, and everyone has one worth learning.

I used to be a job collector: I wanted to meet one person from every job. If I was in a bar or a restaurant, I would talk to the staff to find out their names and one thing about them. With the people having a drink, I would ask their name and their job.

It took me a very long time to meet a plane handler – I probably said the name of the job wrong, but I mean the person who holds the two orange flashlights and makes sure that planes go left or right and don't crash into each other on the runway. The guy didn't feel like his job was important, but it is to me.

I was very excited to meet him – probably too excited, because after five years of searching I had finally met one to add to my collection. Being a job collector was a way for me to get excited about everyone I met.

Just by finding a way to remember people and become excited about them, you are creating a "call back", so when you come back the next day you can say, "Hey Sarah, how are your kids?" At the first bar where I learned how to do this, one of the girls had pet rats, so I would ask about her rats – even though I struggled to understand why someone would keep pet rats.

This is an easy way to form relationships. Most people in the service industry are treated like garbage. Most customers don't remember the waitress's name unless they are trying to get her phone number. Most people treat the bathroom attendant guy like he's human garbage. Do you think he's working his dream job? Do you want that job? If you treat people with respect, they can do unbelievable things for you.

CLIMB THE LADDER

People have different levels of power, and you can work your way up. You go to your favorite restaurant or country club and start at the bottom of the staff. You start with the guy who parks your car, or the person who takes your coat, or the person in the bathroom. You start with the bar backs and then talk to the bartender.

You just meet each person, and you have each person introduce you to someone else. You get the waitress to introduce you the other waitresses. "Hey Sally, you have been an amazing waitress, my family will be coming back here all the time. I really had a good time, but it's possible that I'll have another waitress next time; would you introduce me to a different waitress so when I have a different one they know you served me first? So that if I come here and you are working she knows I have a loyalty to you." Sally will introduce you to the other waitresses and you will have a little more cache than their other customers (and additionally you have to tip well).

Part of this process is just down to "don't be a bad customer; you want to be a positive memory". So then you meet the other waitresses, waiters or other staff, and eventually someone will introduce you to the manager. The manager says, "Oh, you're such a good customer, you are so friendly. Not the most high-paying customer, but you tip very well. Let me introduce you to the owner."

The owner will then say, "Hey, I've heard you have been coming in a lot, all of my people have been talking about you as a good customer and that's really sweet."

Then you can say, "Hey, I just wanted you to know that your waitresses and your managers do a great job. When you have a great team, that is the sign of a great leader, and I wanted to let you know that when someone runs their business right, I respect that. The fact that your team works so hard means that you're a good person."

POPULAR IN THIRTY SECONDS

What you are doing is giving value – you are making their team feel good because when you walk out of there, the boss is going to walk up to each person and go, "That customer said you guys are awesome, I am proud of you." It doesn't cost you anything to treat people right, to do good things, and it's OK to give people a little bit of love – people do hard jobs and do you know what, being appreciated feels really good.

When I was working in retail, if someone said to my manager that I had done a good job, it would make me feel nice. "Wow, someone cared enough to say a word about me!"

Not only that – you have now built a relationship all the way up and you are friends with the owner. Now every time you go in, you can talk to the owner or the chef. You can do some pretty interesting things with restaurants that aren't that fancy. Maybe it's a chain restaurant where they don't have a chef but calls everyone "cooks" or "line cooks", and they have different cook ranks.

One of my friends used to be in this job. He had this amazing thirty-minute story about why the buffalo chicken sandwich was the ultimate product for a restaurant – why it was maximum profit and minimum effort.

I memorized this story because I thought it was brilliant and I could share it with other chefs to show them I am friends with a cook. My friend eventually moved into the IT industry after three or four years, but at this time he was a line cook in a very well-known restaurant.

Even in a chain restaurant, I will ask who made my sandwich and for them to be brought out and say, "Look, I know that you cooked from a recipe but I have been to a lot of these restaurants and you do a really good job, and I want to thank you personally."

People sometimes do it in really fancy restaurants, but it doesn't happen so much in real life – we mostly see it on TV. If you are in a restaurant that is crazy expensive and it is a celebrity chef, it doesn't have the same effect.

If it's that kind of place, here is something really sneaky you can do; you say, "Excuse me, who made my salad?" It's probably going to be the lowest person in the restaurant, and you ask for them to be brought out and say, "Hey dude, this is your first day and what you did to this salad – you are a damn salad magician, it's unbelievable! I have been to this place a dozen times, you crushed it tonight!"

Nobody ever brings out one of the secondary chefs, and that

person will probably remember you forever. All you did was make someone feel good, and that is the entire secret to networking. Treat people the way you want to be treated. Yeah, it's the golden rule – surprise!

Whatever place you choose – whether it is a repeat visit or a one-off venue – this is your strategy. You go in when it's not crowded so it's easier to make connections; you tip well; you treat people with respect; you give them compliments and you learn their name and one thing about them, so every time you see them you can say, "Hey Joe, how's law school going?" "Hey Tony, how's your dog doing?" "Hey Bill, how's amateur archeology?" People will not like you, they will love you – this is the secret to popularity.

EVENT STRATEGY

Now let's say you have an event. It's the same approach, you just have a limited amount of time to work with. You will need to get to the event early and you will want to be strategic and find different places where you can build value.

If it is an event or a conference at a hotel, which is where most of the conferences I go to are held, go to the hotel two or three days early, meet everyone on staff, meet every person who works there and treat them with respect. Shake hands with them, tell them stories. Find out where all the bathrooms are, find out where all of the exits are.

I am a big believer in architecture.

I know it's boring but I'm not sorry – I had to say it. Knowing where every bathroom in a venue is has made me millions of dollars – I can't tell you how many times someone has turned around and asked where the bathroom is, then of course I go, "Oh, it's right over there."

They come back and say, "Hey man, thanks, no one else knew where the bathroom was." If you are at an event where people go to the conference at a hotel and then go to a different location for dinner, rent a car and be the person to play driver. You're super valuable and you have a captive audience. You can do these little things and implement these little strategies to become the dominant force in a venue.

I have podcast episodes and blog posts with free examples on my website. If you want to hear more examples of these ideas, I have links on the "networking for job seekers" page, where you can see all the relevant blog posts and podcast videos that cover this material.

By being strategic, you can absolutely, positively become the dominant force, even if you are going to be somewhere only for a couple of days. When it is an event, you need to know who you want to network with. Is it the speakers or the people in the backrooms? Then you pay attention to where they intersect.

Most of the people attending the conferences I go to never attend the actual event. Half the people I network with don't even buy tickets – they go to the conference hotel and, sit it in the lobby and go to the parties afterward. They don't actually buy a ticket because they don't need to listen to the speakers – there is no value in that part to them. The other parts are far more valuable to them. That's where I do most of my networking – in the hotel lobby or the hotel bar.

At the last event I went to, I ended up in the presidential suite just by walking past the door and knocking at four in the morning. That led to huge networking. These are the types of things that offer you maximum value and allow you to dominate the venue – knowing who you are looking for, knowing where they intersect, and paying attention.

Most people go in blind and they have no idea, "Oh, I just want to listen to a bunch of the talks." Great! They'll learn a bunch of information, even more than they could possibly implement, and they'll be back where they started in six weeks, after spending a lot of money at the event and without a return on their investment. I want more than that for you.

ACTIVITY

Before you go to the next section, write down your exact strategy. You've already been to a couple places, scoped a few out, cased the joints. I want you to write out a specific strategy. Some steps you are going to take are notes from this section on how you are going to dominate the venue, how you are going to become the most popular person there.

Is it a bar, a restaurant, a cafe, is it a yoga studio?

I don't care what it is, this works everywhere. These tools are universal and they are unstoppable.

You should spend one or two hours working on this exercise. When I write out a strategy, I use Google Maps and I look up the location on the old Internet. I look at some satellite pictures and I look at places nearby the venue.

I want to know everything that a local would know about the place. I like to be absolutely prepared. Imagine you are in one of those casino heist movies – that is the level of preparation. Spend some real time on your strategy before you move on to the next section because we are getting real close to that finish line.

STEP FIVE: LEVERAGE THE POWER
OF INTRODUCTIONS

We have talked over and over again about how the person who introduces you determines your perceived value. If it's someone one step down, it's not a big deal – you're within the standard deviation, if you like scientific terms. If the bar back introduces you to the waitress or to the bartender, that's fine – they are of a similar level. If the bathroom attendant introduces you to the owner of the club, that is too big of a gap. This is why we want to do it one step at a time.

The bathroom attendant is worth treating with respect, but most of the time they are not allowed to leave the bathroom. If they are stuck there all night, they can't do anything for you, they can't introduce you to a lot of people. The same thing is true for the front-door bouncer – they usually work at the door the whole night. The guys who walk the floor inside are different.

Making a connection with the guy at the front door is OK, but he can't introduce you to anyone because he's trapped in a specific location, just like the coat-check girl.

What you can do is talk to the bouncer for a minute and have him introduce you to one of the floor bouncers, or you can have him introduce you to the person who runs the clipboard – the person with the list, if it is a fancier place.

Most people treat bouncers like they are monsters. I'll tell you what – I've been in a club where things got real hairy. I've seen a real down and dirty bar fight. Fortunately, I was not a participant. All those guys most of the people spend their whole lives hating, "Ah, that guy carded me!"

Man was I glad when they rushed in and stopped that bloodbath. Blood going everywhere and teeth were about to start flying out. Believe me; it's just like the police. Everyone acts like they don't want them around, but when you need them, they can't show up fast enough.

I had a friend these bouncers would always hassle. One night, he walked up and tipped the guys twenty bucks and said, "You guys always hassle me and I get it. But I know if there is a fight in there and people start hurting each other, you're going protect everyone. I'm here with my girlfriend tonight, and I like that you keep her safe."

At first, they thought he was joking because no one tips the bouncers – if someone does it's only because they want to get in. But guess what – those guys do a critical job. No one ever thinks about it like this, unless you're a bouncer reading this – hey man, I respect what you do.

RESPECT IS SOCIAL GOLD

For every job, find a way to respect it; find a way to say, "You know what, I could never do that." Then, when you meet people, you can talk about how you respect their jobs. Most people have jobs in retail, catering or something similar.

I couldn't do that, physically. Right now I am in the middle of a high tide. I don't write my books, I dictate my books on a little dock. I normally sit in this little spot, but I'm standing next to it right now because the waves keep hitting it and crashing into the air. I have been walking while I dictate this book and in fact, my back hurts from two hours of walking on this shoddy wooden dock.

I couldn't imagine doing a job that requires standing twelve hours a day; that would destroy me. I worked in retail once, when I was in college, and it was brutal. I don't think I'm too good for that job, nor that job is too good for me. I am not physically good enough to do that kind of work.

Construction worker? Man, how do you do it? It is so amazing to me that people have disdain for jobs that they could never physically do. The surgeon who looks down on the construction worker – are you kidding me? Have you ever tried to use a jackhammer?

I have a friend who is a great construction worker, and he asked me to help him paint a house once. While we were painting a room white, some people walked in and said, "What even happened to this wall?" I can't explain it – I thought all white paint would look the same, but it looked horrible. We took a bunch of pictures and everyone was laughing because I'm like an anti-construction worker. I am so bad at manual labor that everyone thought it was hilarious. It's a vivid memory for me. (I'll try to find the photos we took from that day to share on my blog. I know I have them somewhere...)

If you can switch to this mindset where you have respect rather than disdain for everybody in every position out there, it is very easy to meet people and make them feel good. If you just think, "Do I want this job? Could I do this job? Man, this stuff is hard, no thanks." I am very glad I do what I do, because most jobs out there are hard, and I respect what most people do.

You should do that when you are using the power of introduction and introducing your way up the chain. This way, when you are at that restaurant and those dentists are having their meeting next month, you can ask the owner, "What are those guys doing over there?"

"That's a dentists' meetup, they come here once a month"

"Oh, do you think you can introduce me? I'm actually a dental hygienist, it would be good to meet some people in the same profession."

The owner brings you over and goes, "Hey, this is Sally, she's a dental hygienist. I'm the owner and I thought of introducing you because you guys are in the same field, I thought it would be interesting."

Then those dentists will be like, "Wow, this lady knows the owner – she's got some gravitas, some authority, some power." Far more power than if you just walked up as a total stranger. That is the power of introductions.

This technique works for everyone. If you want to meet a movie star, have their agent or their best friend introduce you. It is far easier than walking up cold and saying "I'm a big fan, can you take a picture with me?"

ACTIVITY

This is the brilliance of introductions, so now that you understand it, write down your chain of introductions. You may have even done part of this in your previous exercise, when you were outlining your casino heist Write down the perfect person to meet and the perfect introducer.

Maybe it's even better to have the owner introduce you to one of the dentists ordering a shot, going, "Hey, this is Sally. She's an awesome dental hygienist, and she is the most popular person who comes in here. You are lucky to meet her – she's one of the most important patrons in this restaurant. You guys spend a lot of money, but Sally is something special."

The dentist is going to go, "My name is Dennis the dentist, let me introduce you to some of my friends." Now you get introduced by one of the dentists to all of the other ones, and he'll go, "Hey guys, the owner said this girl is awesome, now you've got to meet her through me." Now you have got the power of the double introduction.

For your activity, write down your introduction strategy for meeting the people that you want to meet. Even better, if you are really serious about success, write down your introduction ladder.

You can go from bathroom attendant to bar back, bar back to bartender, bartender to waitress, waitress to manager, manager to floor manager or regional manager and you work your way up to owner. Maybe the owner doesn't go there, maybe it's a big chain, but you are still going to work your way up to the top manager on site, and they still have a lot of authority. Write everything down and come up with a bit of a plan.

STEP SIX: GIVE VALUE FIRST

*H*opefully you have already noticed this concept throughout the book, but if you haven't yet, I want you to bring it home.

Always give, never ask.

Whenever I meet someone, I ask how can I help them for their business, how can I help them grow their money, who is their perfect introduction, what can I do for them.

If it is a lower-level person than me, or a person in a different industry than mine – a bartender, a waitress or the owner of a restaurant – I know we are in two totally different worlds, and asking how I can help their business wouldn't make any sense. Instead, I'll say something nice or I'll compliment them, make them feel good, or I'll tip them well. These are ways of giving value.

Telling someone their staff is really wonderful gives value to them and to their staff; remember that's why we do that. That's why we talk that way. I want people to feel good when they do a good job; I want people to feel respected and loved and to feel good about themselves. That's value.

Giving people good times, giving people happiness – that is mostly what I do. That is what networking mostly comes down to: making people feel good in different ways. Being the life of the party, being the kindest person, being the best complimenter – these are all great skills.

You can also be interesting. When I first wanted to learn how to be interesting, I learned how to read palms, and I learned from a woman who did it professionally. The very first bar and restaurant that I dominated, I went in and read everyone's palms when the place was empty.

Now I have a few rules – when I do a palm reading I give everyone a positive reading; I give them a palm reading that makes them feel good. Don't give someone a palm reading or break out the tarot cards and tell them they are going to die; that is the worst thing you could do.

I'm not a big believer in mysticism. I don't believe that palm reading is real, even though I know the rules and I know that there are dozens of different sets of rules because everyone reads palms in a different way. I just focus on giving people a bit of fun.

They know that I'm not serious about it, it's just a little bit myste-rious and it makes them feel good. That's my goal. Then everyone remembers, "Oh, it's palm-reading Jonathan." I don't read palms anymore – it has been years since I've done it, but it was a lot of fun and a very effective way to give value and be remembered.

Some people decide to become magicians, but that's a lot more work. I have some friends that are great magicians. Learning palm reading takes about thirty minutes. You can learn palm-reading online; there are dozens of websites that explain it.

It's just to give you an idea – I don't want every single person who reads this book to go out and read palms. That's not necessary and it can affect how people see you as a professional. I was a musician at the time, so it was kind of okay, as they are two different types of entertainer. You may need to find a fun way to connect with people that is congruent with your career.

HOW CAN I HELP YOU?

You can be interesting or give value and you can say to people, "What can I do for you?" or "How can I help you?" There are so many little things you can do for people that mean a lot. People email all the time to let me know they left a review for one of my books. It seems like a tiny thing, but that really means a lot to me and it gets them onto my radar.

You can say to the owner of the restaurant, "Hey, what would help you the most? Would you like me to write a review on your Facebook page or your Google profile, Yelp or whatever? What can I do? Would it help if I recorded a video?"

This is the same type of approach you can use when you are networking at a conference. You can say to people, "What can I do that would help you? What if I shot a video saying that you're an awesome dentist, a great guy or the best waitress here? What if I shot a video right now and I said Sally is the best waitress? When you come here, ask for Sally!"

I recently hosted an event. As I told you, I threw a party when I was in San Diego. I hired a bar and I rented private security – I am very serious about that. Nothing bad ever happens at my events, and this is because I hire private security.

The security guy I hired was very professional; he did a very excellent job. When I wrote a review for the company, I said, "If you use this company, this is who you have to ask for. This guy is so professional."

We had a few models, lots of very beautiful women, and lots of very wealthy people. We had one incident where someone was uninvited and very unkind to the waitress at the restaurant.

I will tell you right now, I don't care if you are a billionaire, you don't talk to waitresses like they are trash.

This guy had said to this girl, "Do you know who I am? Do you know how important I am? Do you know how I can mess with your career?" My first thought was to tell security to rough the guy up. I know who the guy is – he is very wealthy, but I don't care. You don't talk to people like that and you certainly don't do it under my name.

I said to the waitress, "We rented out this place, and no one talks to you like that." She thought that she was going to be in trouble with me, but no. The guy wasn't invited to the event. He's not someone I am friends with, he just happened to be in my orbit.

Why would I want to do business with someone who talks to people like that? Of course I wouldn't, that's disgusting. The guy already has a terrible reputation for being a terrible person, and I would never do business with someone who treats people like that.

This security guy handled it as good as you could. He got rid of them and made this girl feel safe. She was about to cry because she felt so unsafe both physically and in her career, and that is not OK by me. He did a great job – private security, wearing a suit, looking like a real pro. There were a couple of other smaller things that he handled. I felt like a movie star and I felt like I didn't have to worry about anything – I knew it was handled and I liked that, so I wrote a great review.

What do you think happened to his career when that review popped up? What do you think his boss said? I know for a fact that this guy saw the review. His boss said, "Hey, you've got to see this. I don't know what you did, but this is the best review anyone has ever written."

I worked really hard to be eloquent – I wanted to go the extra mile. All I was doing was giving value. Most people don't ever write reviews – most of the time, I don't write reviews either.

You can do things like this to give people huge value; I don't want anything in return. I don't know if I will ever throw another party when I go to California again. It is very stressful to make sure everyone is having a good time and it kind of wears me out, so I may do different things down the line. But I gave the guy value, not wanting anything in return – he had already done his job. All he had done was his job. You can easily say that he did what I paid him to do.

KILLING WITH KINDNESS

When people do their jobs well, they should be rewarded; they should be treated right and they should be given value. If you can become someone who gives everyone around them value and makes people feel good all the time, you will be excellent at finding amazing jobs and you will make a lot more money. All you have to do is become a complimenter.

When I wanted to learn how to make friends, I studied a guy named Nathan – you might have read this story in other books and other places, but I want to share it again.

He was the first person I met in my life who was both popular and kind. I still wonder these days if part of it was that he had a terrible memory. Every time I saw him, he would come up and he would go, "Oh my gosh Jonathan, I love that sweatshirt!"

He complimented the same sweatshirt, in the same way, four or five times. For a while, I thought he was teasing me. I was so used to mean people, but he wasn't one. I don't know where the path of his life has taken him – it was long before Facebook– but I learned the power of treating people nicely from him. Everyone liked him, and I don't think it was a strategy – I think it was who he was as a person.

He would start every conversation with a compliment and I would love to say that I am perfect at this, but I am not. I'm actually quite an introvert – it's only when I'm proactively networking that I actually do this.

Most of the time, I'm with my wife and children and I stay within my tight circle, but when I leave my island it's time to network. I try to compliment people, I try to make people feel good, I try to give people value. I learned this lesson when I was seventeen, and learning how to make friends is the secret to popularity.

I am friends with people who are total nerds, but they always say something nice, and that's enough. Nothing else matters. I am also friends with professional athletes, Olympic athletes, well-known musicians and famous actors. All of that comes down to treating people right, so they want to be around you. If you don't, then I don't.

ACTIVITY

Practice giving value for the next week. Write down creative compliments and ways you can give value to each person on the "introduction ladder" you wrote in the previous activity.

We are close to having a complete blueprint for networking success and getting you closer to your ideal target. You now have your target, the location, the people you need to connect with, and how you will give them value. We are close to the finish line.

STEP SEVEN: PLANT SEEDS

*I*t's time to bring it all home: this is the final step. You have made it to the finish line and I am proud of you. Here's how this works.

How do you let people know you are looking for a job without becoming desperate?

It's like that old adage every man suffers from – no one wants you until you have a girlfriend, then suddenly everyone likes you. If you become single again, no one wants you again. The same thing applies to jobs – if you have been out of work for too long, people start to see you as toxic. They'll think if no one has hired you, you must be unhirable. You don't want that.

I've already shared this lesson with you, but let's bring it home again. I want to remind you because it's very critical: "Hey, I'm not looking for work right now, but I am always open to cool opportunities." That's what you want to say.

"I'm a CPA, I'm always looking for something interesting to work on. I want to work on something I am passionate about, or work with a company. I am passionate about. If you've got anything, I'm interested."

That is the way we plant a seed, and planting seeds is all you've got to do. People say to me, "How do you get so many projects?" I've never bid on a ghostwriting job, I've never posted on a forum, I don't need any of that stuff because I use networking to build my business.

I say to everyone in my social circle, "I'm not taking on new clients right now unless it's something really interesting." Or, "I'm looking for an interesting new project to work on."

I plant this little seed with everyone and it is the same thing as answering the question, "What kind of person do you want to meet?" It's a similar thing: "What type of project are you looking for?"

You say, "Hey, let me know if you hear of any jobs like this."

"Let me know if you hear about any dental jobs."

"Let me know if you hear of any jobs in the IT department."

"Let me know if you hear of anything with this kind of opening."

"I might be looking for something cool, I'm taking a little time off."

"I've taken some time off, I am doing a little bit of consulting right now, but might want to go back in house – I'm thinking about it."

Do you see what you are doing there? You're planting seeds. This is how you let people know you are looking for a job without catching that stigma.

Let everyone know what you are looking for, and whichever type of networking you're doing, if you plant those seeds eventually they'll grow to fruition.

Sometimes you share Skype details with someone and nothing comes of it. Out of every ten deals I set up at an event, about one comes through in the short term.

Sometimes six months later, a year or even two years later, they'll message me and go, "Hey, I remember what you said. Something big came up and we need a ghostwriter for a big job. It's outside of what we normally do, but can we make it happen?" It's done, it's there. That's the power.

The more you plant seeds, the more they will grow. You don't need to worry about them in the short term. Plant the seeds and let it lie. "Hey, this is what I do. I'm always open for new, interesting and cool projects." We wrote down your seed earlier, so you've already got it. "Hey, I'm a dental hygienist; I'm looking for…I don't know, something cool. I want to work in the right kind of environment – culture is so important. Having the right thing with the dentist on the other team, it's so important." So something comes up and it's really interesting, like a Rock 'n Roll dentist, or a fifties themed dentists, or a space station themed dentist. I don't know if these exist, but they sound really fun to me.

ACTIVITY

That's how we plant our seeds, so for your final activity, write down your exact seed phrase. You might need to write down three or four variations of it. Lock it down and then start planting it.

Does everyone in your life know what type of job you are looking for? Have you planted the seed with people you already know, that are already in your social network? Start doing it.

Write down your action steps and plan your implementation. Start taking action.

THE END OF THE ROAD

*Y*ou've made it to the final section. Your journal is full of things you need to do and now it's all about implementation. I have given you a great deal of information, hopefully it hasn't been overwhelming. What you need to do now, is take that action and do it.

If you read this entire book and you never actually wrote down anything, you never actually put together a job seeker journal, you will probably forget everything in about two weeks.

This is the part of the book where I would ask you to leave me a great review, but if you didn't do any of the exercises, then this system probably won't work for you. If you did – if you found this helpful, if you took action, if you implemented it, then click on that fifth star and leave me a good review. It helps me to help other job seekers. It helps me to build my business, feed my kids, take care of my family – that would mean a lot to me. It's a way you can give me value like I've given you value through this book.

You are probably wondering how that job interview from the start of the book went – of course I got the job. It was not my dream job, but I thought it was at the time. I eventually realized that my destiny was to work for myself, but at twenty-nine I was the head of a department with a one point five million dollar budget and six other teachers with more experience than me and far older than me.

Out of thirty people in my master's class, I was the only one to get a university position in one of the top universities in America. Beyond that, it was a position where I was teaching, while running a department and I was in charge of other teachers.

It is possible to use these techniques to give value, to be strategic, and to get amazing jobs. At the time, that university job wasn't posted anywhere. They said, "We have a job, we haven't announced it or posted it anywhere, but you sent in a cold email and you sound very interesting – let's talk." That's how you can plant those seeds and be proactive. I want you to be an action-taker and I want you to have success. This isn't a book about ideas; this is a book about action steps. It is an instruction manual. The only way an instruction manual works is if you actually do the steps.

Now it is time for you to take action on the steps. Go forth into the world and actually get that better job you deserve!

You can find me on LinkedIn and you can message me or send me an email – I would love to hear about you getting a new position or see a picture. That stuff gives a lot of value and a lot of love to me.

I want to help you in your career, but the ball is in your court now. I have carried you this far, now it is your turn – it is your chance to carry the rest of the way. We are a team, we have done something amazing together and I have shared with you my most successful tactics for networking. This is how you can get this next job!

Even if you haven't lost your job yet, it is time to start building that network now. The techniques we talk about in the real world apply digitally as well. When you meet people online, offer them value by saying nice things to them. Treat them well and build that network, so when you need a job or are in between appointments or you need to bring in some consulting work, the network is there, ready to carry you.

Take action now, and your network will always be there for you.

DID YOU JOIN YET?

*I*t's not too late. You get one last chance to go beyond this book. If you have questions and want to connect, the Tribe is where all of that happens. Books are no longer one-way streets. We can chat back and forth. If you are stuck on any of the seven steps, ask in the group!

We are waiting for you to join us!

https://servenomaster.com/NetworkingInvite

MORE INFORMATION

*T*hroughout this book I mentioned other books, images, links, and additional content. All of that can be found at:

ServeNoMaster.com/NetworkingForJobseekers

YOU DON'T HAVE to worry about trying to remember any other links or the names of anything mentioned in this book. Just enjoy the journey and focus on taking control of your destiny.

FOUND A TYPO?

While every effort goes into ensuring that this book is flawless, it is inevitable that a mistake or two will slip through the cracks.

If you find an error of any kind in this book, please let meets know by visiting:

ServeNoMaster.com/typos

I appreciate you taking the time to notify me. This ensures that future readers never have to experience that awful typo. You are making the world a better place.

ABOUT THE AUTHOR

Born in Los Angeles, raised in Nashville, educated in London - Jonathan Green has spent years wandering the globe as his own boss - but it didn't come without a price. Like most people, he struggled through years of working in a vast, unfeeling bureaucracy. And even though he was 'totally crushed' when he got fired, it gave him the chance to reappraise his life and rebuild it from scratch.

Since 2010, he's been making a full-time living on the Internet - helping brick and mortar business owners promote themselves on the Internet, helping men and women find true love, ghostwriting best sellers for some of the biggest publishers in the world and much, much more.

Thanks to smart planning and personal discipline, he was more successful than he could have possibly expected. He traveled the world, helped friends and family, and moved to an island in the South Pacific.

Now he's passing his knowledge onto the rest of the world as host of a weekly podcast that teaches financial independence, networking with the world's most influential people, writing epic stuff online, and traveling the world for cheap.

His hobbies include kayaking, surfing, and building empires. He currently has a loving girlfriend, and two wonderful kids who love the ocean (almost!) as much as he does.

Find out more about Jonathan at:

ServeNoMaster.com

ONE LAST THING

Reviews are the lifeblood of any book on Amazon and especially for the independent author. If you would click five stars on your Kindle device or visit this special link at your convenience, that will ensure that I can continue to produce more books. A quick rating or review helps me to support my family and I deeply appreciate it.

Without stars and reviews, you would never have found this book. Please take just thirty seconds of your time to support an independent author by leaving a rating.

Thank you so much!

To leave a review go to ->

https://servenomaster.com/jobreview

Sincerely,
Jonathan Green
ServeNoMaster.com

Made in the USA
San Bernardino, CA
23 January 2018